Choosing a Dog Breed Guide

How to Choose the Right Dog for You

Eric Nolah

Choosing A Dog Breed Guide
by Eric Nolah

ISBN 978-0-9866004-5-6

Printed in the United States of America

Copyright © 2010 Psylon Press

Version 1.1

Also by Eric Nolah

Dog Breeds Pictures
ISBN 978-0-9866004-6-3

Cute Puppy Pictures
ISBN 978-0-9866004-7-0

Contents

Forward

Having a dog as a pet is not always the right thing for many people. Some people can't stand the thought of having a dog, while others don't like the idea of having to clean up after their dog.

The people who do love to have a dog as their pet and bosom companion are the people who will devote the most time, energy and effort into raising their dog.

These people will find that their lives are empty without a dog to fill in the void and will almost always have at least one dog with them. I am I have to say, one of these people.

I got my first dog when I was nine years old and I haven't looked back since. In the way of children all over the world, I pleaded and begged and all but sold my soul to get my first dog, and then proceeded to forget all about him as the novelty wore off in the first few months.

The dog, Catcher, however didn't forget me and continued to faithfully dog my steps (excuse the pun) until without my even realizing it, he took up a large portion of my affection.

I was lucky in this, my first dog lived to the ripe old age of twelve, whereupon he succumbed to old age and went to doggy heaven.

After a suitable period of mourning I then found myself missing the unquestioning loyalty and faithfulness of my soul companion so I went searching around for another companion.

This wasn't as easy as I thought since I didn't want another Labrador (Catcher was a Labrador), but then again I didn't want to deviate too far from the doggy characteristics that made Catcher my dog-in-a-million.

Amazingly enough, unlike when I went looking for Catcher for the first time at age nine, I found that mature college student that I was, I was still having difficulty finding and choosing the right dog for me.

I spent hours trawling through the various books and other magazines about dogs, in an effort to find out what I needed to know before I made a decision.

Being older I now needed some specific characteristics from my dog, traits which Catcher innately had, or which he learned through interaction with me as the years wore on.

But since this was a whole new ball game, and a whole different breed of dog I was after, I gave the matter more thought than I otherwise might have.

This in turn led to my ultimately embracing everything that was dog, which in turn has led me to this point.

I have seen so many mismatched pairings of owner and dog over the years troop in and out of my sight that I finally gave in to the pleadings of my best friend and decided to put down on paper what knowledge I have collected, with the thought of helping fellow dog lovers to find the best pairing of dog for them.

Of course with the advent of the internet it has become much easier to find help in choosing the right dog breed for you, but even there I have found that you have to do a little bit of legwork before you can get to heart of the matter.

Here, with this book, I have tried to give you as much knowledge and help as I could to get along with the little matter of choosing your perfect-fit dog.

I don't claim to have everything written down on these pages that you should know about dogs and selecting the correct dog.

Nor have I managed to find information about each and every type of dog that exists in the world today. That would be an almost never-ending impossible task what with the different cross bred dogs which abound.

However, there is a goodly amount of information for you to take, and which will hopefully be of help to you.

Oh, yes. You might also be interested in knowing that I now have a spunky four year old Chihuahua and a six month old Saint Bernard that admittedly tends to slobber over everything. And overseeing this odd pairing, I have an eight year old Labrador whom I found in an animal shelter.

Introduction

It's never easy having to let go of a beloved family pet and this holds true whether your pet is of the mammalian variety, the reptilian variety, the insect variety, or the bird variety. A family pet is a family and that's that.

Actually that's not all. A family pet is so much more than "that's that". A family pet is to all intents and purposes, another family member. And that's where finding the right pet to suit you and your lifestyle is of the utmost importance.

This can apply to most any animal that you decide to take on as a pet, but to me, I feel this holds especially true if you're looking at having a dog as a pet.

It's true that birds and other pets can form an attachment to you, but a dog I feel, forms more of a bond with its owner. After all, they're not called "man's best friend" for nothing.

The bond you form with your dog can be as deep and lasting as any other bond that you form with your family members. In some cases, it can go even deeper still, and this has been demonstrated time and again over the years.

"Lassie" the movie, might only be a corny much overdone movie to many people, but at heart it is true, and embodies the spirit of the bond between owner and dog.

To that extent it becomes imperative that you decide upon which type of dog you want in your life before you actually go and adopt one. This is where this book comes in handy.

You can use the facts I've mentioned in this book to help get a start in deciding which breed of dog will suit you.

You also then have the additional option of being able to investigate further on your own, and even take a look, at the different types of dogs that interest you.

You will find in this book most of the information that you need to help you choose the right breed of dog for you. As far as possible I have placed the information in an orderly manner to make it easier for you to go through and help you find your dog.

And on a little side note, you will find that at various points in this book that I have referred to the dogs as "he". This is for no other reason than I have had mostly male dogs, and that I have become used to referring to them as "he".

And even when I caught on to this fact it was still easier for me to go on referring to the dog in male terms. I found that introducing a "she" term into the mix just muddied up the waters for me when I was writing.

For that reason, I have referred to the dog either as "it", or as "he".

Are You Ready to Own a Dog?

This is the first question that you need to ask yourself.

Contrary to what many people might believe, this is one of the more important questions that you must answer before getting a dog.

This is the reason why I have placed this particular section before the next section on how to go about "Choosing the Right Dog for you".

Here, more so even than in the other section you will need to be brutally truthful and honest with yourself because the answers you give here will necessarily affect your choices later on.

The Questions & Answers

There are no right or wrong answers to any of these questions. They are simply a means which can be used to help you decide whether or not you really are ready for a dog and all the consequences that go along with it.

So what are these questions that you will need to answer? Simply,

- Do you really want a dog

- Do you have the time to spare on a dog

- Are you willing to provide companionship

- Do you have the patience necessary to deal with your dog

- Is your family ready to deal with a dog

- Is your family going to help with the training

- Who is going to be responsible for the dog

- Can you really live with a dog underfoot and in the house all the time

- Is money going to be a problem

- What are your long term plans

The answers, which are really not answers as such, but are more of explanations and clarifications on what you need to think of, are as follows.

Do You Really Want a Dog?

The first and most important question, is whether you really want a dog. Many people mistakenly believe that a dog is all fun, they don't consider all the hard work and effort that goes into raising a dog.

So, do you want a dog just for the fun of it, to keep you company, or are you able to give it its due and tend to it and look after its needs for what amounts to the rest of its natural life?

Here again many people will get their dog and then find that the hassle is not worth the effort and will give the dog away, most of the time to a pound or a shelter or similar place.

You need to decide whether you really want a dog or not. The responsibility aspect of the whole thing aside, is this just a passing fancy, or do you really want to have dog.

This is a very serious question, and there is no "of course" about it. Just because you say that you want a dog, it doesn't necessarily follow that you *want* a dog.

If you think that it will help, you can go through this book to find out whether or not a dog is the right choice for you.

The book might be about choosing the right dog for you, but it can also help to clarify in your mind whether you are ready to deal with all the complications that a dog will bring to your life.

Don't get me wrong, I'm not trying to put you off getting a dog, I think they are the perfect friends and companions for many people, but not everyone is equipped to deal with a dog in their lives.

So give the dog its due, and yourself a break, and think this through very seriously before getting a dog.

Do You Have the Time to Spare for a Dog?

This is one of the crucial questions that you will have to ask of yourself if you're thinking about getting a dog for yourself,

In the initial stages soon after you get your dog, whether you get a full grown dog or a puppy, you will need to sped time with him in order to get him used to the way things are supposed to be.

You may have to leave him for hours on end at times if you need to go to work, but that shouldn't be taken as a license to completely ignore your new companion.

You might be tired and thinking about only your bed, but your dog will need to be tended to as well, besides which they will have been waiting eagerly for you to get back so that they can spend their time with you.

This is especially true in the early days when you're a stranger to the dog, and the territory and surroundings are also new and unfamiliar. A puppy especially will need extra attention if it is to be weaned successfully from its mother.

The time that you devote to your dog in this stage will however be time that is well worth the effort. You will reap much of what you sow in this time period over the many years that you spend with your dog.

If you play your cards right in this stage of your friendship, you will find that you have a loyal and faithful friend and companion for life.

Are You Willing to Provide the Companionship?

Are you willing to provide the companionship that is necessary for the dog to be happy? This is important as, if you are not willing to devote at least a portion of your time everyday on your dog, he will become unhappy.

Not everyone is willing to expend their energies on keeping a canine companion happy. This is something that you need to look into quite seriously especially if you don't have other dogs or pets.

Dogs are, from their very nature sociable animals and many require constant loving care and attention.

Just about all dogs however, will need nothing more strenuous from you than your warm body next to theirs as you go about your business. You need to be willing to provide this to them on at least some level in order to have a successful rapport with your dog.

You don't *have* to let them slobber all over you if you don't want to, but a loving pat on the head, a sincere, "Good boy!", and a reward biscuit or two at odd moments will let them know that you care about them and that you're thinking about their welfare.

There are of course, some dogs that don't need this loving care and attention in spades, so if you are still considering getting yourself a dog, and you don't want to devote all your attentions on your dog, then I suggest that you look into getting this type of dog.

Do You Have the Patience Necessary?

Another crucial factor when you're thinking about getting a dog is whether you have the right temperament to deal with you new dog. This question goes hand in hand with the earlier one of whether you have the time needed to devote to it.

A puppy will necessarily need to be given much time as well as care and attention if you're to train it properly.

It's no use thinking that you need to train it and keep putting it off, only to find out one year later that your cute little puppy has developed bad habits, is not properly house trained, refuses to come when you call him, and that he has destructive tendencies to boot.

You will need to train the puppy, and you will need to hold on to your patience by a thread sometimes, but getting mad and punishing the puppy harshly for something that comes naturally to it, is just not the way to go.

If you constantly do this and lose your patience with the puppy, you will find that you have an ill-behaved dog who doesn't respond to anything other than fear.

If you get a full grown dog, unless that dog has been trained properly, you will need to go through its paces and train it the way it should have been trained in the first place.

The old adage, "You can't teach an old dog new tricks" most definitely does not apply here. You *can* teach an old dog new tricks, it just takes time, effort and lots of patience on your part.

So if you are thinking about getting a full grown dog, either get one that has been trained and knows the ways of the human world, or be prepared to have to spend the time to train it the way you want.

Is Your Family Ready for a Dog?

If you have family members living with you, you need to find out if they are alright with having a dog in the house and underfoot all the time.

If all of your family members are not completely happy with the idea of having a dog as a pet, you need to discuss things with them before getting your dog.

It's no use getting a dog on the basis that maybe your family will become used to having the dog and therefore accept it warmly and with open arms later on.

Who knows, they might take an instant dislike to the dog in which case you will need to some kind of action. So you do need to discuss things with your family and come to a decision before getting a dog.

It's not fair for any of you – the dog included – if you ignore the basic likes and dislikes of your family. Everyone needs to be happy, and this is something that you need to take into consideration.

Dogs are sensitive beings and know when all is not right with the world around them. If there is much disharmony in the family the dog will also feel it, and will react to it. You will be able to notice this in a lessening of the dog's spirits and odd behavior that was not noticeable earlier.

Is Your Family Going to Help?

Another thing that goes along with the earlier question, is how much is your family willing to go along with in the training of the dog. Are they going to get to a side and let you do it alone? Or will they chip in and help you?

This is fine and will in no way cause any trouble to you or your dog unless you expressly wanted their cooperation, or conversely wanted them to keep their distance.

But if, in their helpfulness, your family members are sending out mixed signals to your dog, you might find that when you tell your dog to "come here", that it rolls over and plays dead instead. Obviously this is not what you want!

Again, all I can say is that you do need to discuss things with your family first, and even after getting your dog, you need to make sure that everyone is on the same page as you are.

I realize this might be difficult at times, but if things are getting difficult on the home front, you will find that your dog will also feel this and like I said earlier, react to it.

Who is Responsible for the Dog?

You will also need to decide early on who is going to be responsible for the dog. If you're the one who's getting the dog, fine.

But if you're getting the dog for your children, then you need to set some ground rules from the beginning itself, and then expect that you will have to do the majority of cleaning, feeding and general looking after of the dog.

This is the way of children, and something that you need to accept when you give in to your kids and say "Okay, you can have a dog".

You know your kids and you know that ultimately you will have to be the primary caregiver to the dog, despite any eager assurances to the contrary, so you need to be prepared to deal with that and deal with the dog and all of its needs as well.

This means that when you give in to your kids and go to get a dog, you are tacitly agreeing to take on the responsibility.

And even if your kids give you the surprise of a lifetime and take on the full responsibility for the dog, you will still need to be their rock in a storm and be there for them if something goes wrong.

In other words, you need to be ready to step in and shoulder the responsibility for the dog, at the drop of a hat.

Can You Really Live with a Dog in the House?

Are you alright with the idea that your dog will be underfoot most of the time? That it will most likely choose to spend most of its time indoors rather than outdoors, even if you do have a backyard the size of the Grand Canyon?

As I mentioned earlier, dogs are sociable animals, and need and prefer the company of their human buddies more than you might imagine.

This means that not only will you have to find a place for it to stay indoors when you are at home, you might also have to face a few destructive tantrums in the early days when you and your dog are still sniffing out your boundaries.

There are of course exceptions to this rule and you will be able to find a few dogs that don't mind a solitary existence, but they are few and far between, and might not be of the cute and cuddly variety that you're looking for.

Is Money Going to be a Problem?

Unlike in the days of old, caring for a dog has become more expensive. And the bigger or more needy the dog, the more you will need to spend out of hand on the well being of your dog.

You will find that some people go an extra mile and take their dogs to professional services such as professional groomers. You don't need to do this but it something that you want to consider.

You might also find that you want to take out doggy medical insurance in the event that your dog needs to have major surgery or something like that.

Then you also have the normal veterinary bills that you will need to foot if you don't have doggy medical insurance, as well as the cost of medicines and injections etc., which are needed.

Then there's always the chance that you will have to pay damages to any property that your dog has wreaked (or wrecked!) havoc on.

Or you will need to have third party insurance or something similar in the event that your dog just ups and bites someone.

It might not be the dog's fault and he might have been mightily provoked, but you will still be liable for any problems that arise from this.

And then there's the cost of food, grooming items, toys and numerous other little bits and pieces that you will have to take into account when you're totting up the amount you will need to spend on your dog.

These will all ultimately add up over the days, months and years, and is something that you need to think about if you're going to get a dog.

Most of these monetary concerns are long term ones that you should factor into your reckoning before proceeding any further. I have gone into slightly greater detail in the section "The amount of money you're willing to spend".

What Are Your Long Term Plans?

The same applies to your long term plans house-wise. If you need to move for any reason, either work related or otherwise life-related, you will need to think of what you to do with your dog.

Are you going to be able to take the dog with you, can you keep the dog with a trusted neighbor, friend or family member, or do you have the ability to keep him somewhere for the duration that you are away?

What If You Need to Make a Permanent Move Out of the Country?

Can you take your dog with you, what are the laws governing that country about bringing in dogs, and most importantly can your dog live in that particular climate.

A husky for instance might find tropical temperatures to be too hard for it to tolerate, just as it will difficult for some large dogs like the Saint Bernard to acclimatize itself to hot climes as well.

You will obviously be unable to predict the future, but if there is a change of venue in your foreseeable future, you will definitely want to take that into account.

Choosing the Right Dog for You...

If you're new to the game and have never had a dog before, or even if you have had a dog before, you will find that it's not the easiest thing in the world to choose a new dog for you.

You can go through many pet stores and you can trawl through the many books and magazines like I did in an effort to get to the heart of the matter of finding the right dog for you, but in the end, it is still a difficult prospect.

I'm not saying that just because you read through this book that you will be able to magically decide which type of dog you want, but it does help, that much I can say with confidence.

There are many things that you might want to look into before choosing a dg, but I can assure that some of the most basic questions have been looked into in this section.

So before you jump right into the deep end and decide straight off the bat that you want a particular breed of dog, you might first want to go through this small checklist that I have included below.

This will help you in determining what breed of dog best suits your needs and your lifestyle. This latter aspect is a very important one as it will be very difficult for you to keep a dog that is high-maintenance if your own life is not geared to such an effort.

You will need to make sure that your resources, your lifestyle and personal preferences all match up before getting the right dog for you.

It's all well and good to rescue a puppy from the pound that needs rescuing, or even adopt a dog from one of the many animal shelters, but unless you're able to take care of the dog in the manner to which it should be treated, you will only be subjecting yourself and the dog to more trouble.

So think twice and even thrice before giving in to your kids' pleading eyes, or your own sympathetic heart, and find out beforehand whether that cute little Afghan Collie you saw the other day, will fit into your lifestyle, or whether you can live the rest of your life with the pleading eyes of a Basset Hound staring at you.

There are of course other considerations which you must take into account, but these are undoubtedly the most important ones. They are,

- Your lifestyle

- Your available resources

- Your personal preference

Once you sort through these you will then need to get to grips with the other just as important, niggling little details before you should even think about getting yourself a dog.

You could if you want, skip through this next section and get to the part about the dogs, but then again you should also keep in mind that that is how many a dog has ended up at an animal shelter or a pound.

Good intentions and soft heart notwithstanding, if you and your dog don't suit each other, there's going to be more trouble and heartache all around than either of you bargained for.

The same applies if the dog isn't intended for you, but for your children. It is a fact of life that just about all children will go through the stage where they want to have a pet.

This can of course span any number of animals and insects, ranging from pet snakes to pet hamsters to pet cockroaches.

The problem that you get in just about all of these cases is when the novelty of having a pet wears off for your child and the responsibilities come crashing in.

That's when you will find yourself the proud owner of a pet cobra, tarantula, hamster, frog or even a beetle.

And that's when you will find yourself having to brave your fear or dislike of the cobra or the cockroach to take care of it, because naturally you don't want to have to face the accusing eyes of your child because you were so heartless as to let it die.

The same thing applies to a dog. If you're getting one for the benefit of your children you should be fully prepared to take on the responsibility of having to feed it, walk it and generally look after it.

So go through the questions in the next section carefully and by the time that you get to the end of the book, you should have a better idea of what you're facing.

Towards the end of book I have also included a small section on the various basic needs that you will have to look after in your dog.

I included this section purely because to me at least, it follows that if you went about the matter of choosing the right dog for you, you should also know what to do with said dog!

What You Should Ask Yourself

Below is the list of questions which you should think about asking yourself before you get a dog.

You need to answer them as truthfully as you are able to as this will better help you go through the process of finding the right dog for you. If you don't have the time or the energy to devote to a dog full time, that's alright.

As long as you are fully aware of this fact and can accept it for yourself without feeling any guilt or remorse, you can then go about finding a dog for you.

All that is required from you here is to answer the questions to the best of your abilities and not mislead yourself. Remember, this is not an exam so you don't need to rush through it or finish it within a certain time frame.

Take your time and think things over carefully. The more thought you give to some of the questions the better.

If you're not sure what, or even how, you need to answer some of the questions (you are after all going through this whole thing to *help* you find a dog), you might want to think about taking a trip to your local pet store for some inspiration.

Of course, if you are going to do that, you might want to leave your checkbook, wallet, credit cards and anything resembling money, behind at home so that you don't give in to temptation and pleading large brown eyes!

I can tell you from firsthand experience that it is amazingly difficult to resist big brown puppy eyes staring soulfully up at you through their glass enclosure.

If you're taking a stroll to the pet store or animal shelter or other such place, there is a little something else that you should leave behind, along with your wallet: your children.

It's almost guaranteed that if you take your children along with you to scout out the dogs before deciding on what type of dog you want, you will end up coming home with something that you don't want, can't handle, and definitely have no way of looking after.

So keep the children home, but do bring along your will power. If you've already made the decision to get a dog, then there's a good chance that you will succumb to impulse anyway, and have a certain dog, or puppy kept on hold especially for you until you can pop back to your house for your wallet!

I have seen this happen time and again. Don't do it. The best thing that you can do for yourself, your children if you have any, and the dog you want to get, is to evaluate your choices before making a decision.

Haste and impulse decisions never make for comforting bedfellows and I can assure you that if you get a dog with the obedience capability of a flea, you will definitely be sharing your bed with the dog!

After going through this section you can then go on to the next section and go through a few of the different dog breeds available for you to look into which I have included in the book more as a guideline so that you know what you're looking for.

I have posed the questions first, so that you can get a general idea of what you're looking for. I have then gone through them in greater detail afterwards to give you a better idea of what you need to think about.

- The size of the dog

- Where will the dog be housed

- Do you want an active dog, or a couch potato

- The amount of time you're willing to spend on grooming

- What type of coat would you prefer – long or short

- The amount of money you're willing to spend

- Are you going to train the dog

- Is exercising the dog going to be a problem

- Is the dog going to be left alone for most of the day

- How much space – yard space etc. – do you have to spare

- Do you have children, especially young babies or toddlers

- Do you have other pets

- Why do you want a dog

- Have you ever owned a dog before this

- Are you looking for special traits and characteristics in your dog

- Where do you live – climate-wise that is

- Are you looking for a purebred dog, or a mixed breed dog

- The cuteness factor

- Are you allergic to dogs

The Size of the Dog

When asked whether they want a small sized dog or a large sized dog, most people will waffle a bit, but some will be able to tell you straight off whether they want something the size of a Chihuahua or a Saint Bernard or something in between.

For those of you who are unfamiliar with the different breeds and therefore unfamiliar with the various different sizes, this can be confusing. After all, the Chihuahua could be the bigger of the two and the Saint Bernard only as big as a large hamster.

Since this is not the case, if you don't know the relative size of a breed of dog, don't attempt to quantify your answer using a dog breed as an identifier.

Instead, use a distinct size, like height. You can be sure that there will be at least one or two (dozen!) dogs breeds out there that fit the bill for your sizing needs.

If on the other hand, you do know what the different dog sizes are, you can easily give an example citing these various dogs.

The other thing that you might not want to do when deciding on the size you prefer to have in your dog, is to say that you would like a dog that is large, or small, or smallish, or largish, or medium sized.

What are these sizes, really? Your idea of medium could vary greatly from my idea of what a medium sized dog should look like, and your large could be miles away from what I consider to be large. You could very easily end up with a Boxer when what you really wanted was a Collie.

So be specific when you're deciding on a relative size, or as specific as you can be, and work within those bounds. Whatever you do, avoid using such vague terms as "small", "medium", "large", and everything else in between.

Since not all dogs are the same, just because you get a small dog, it is not a guarantee that it will be happy to stay cooped up inside your small apartment all day long.

Some small dogs are eminently unsuitable for this, whereas some larger dogs will prefer the cozy surroundings and not complain too much at the cramped living space.

You might find yourself tripping over him, but you an be assured that he will love all the attention he's getting!

Don't just stop at this first question though, thinking that it solves all your dog choosing needs. Go through the rest of the questions and you will see how some needs are closely intertwined with each other and how one answer that you give in one section could be contradicted in another part.

This is the fun of going through this checklist, and you will find that by the time you're done with the whole thing, that you have formed a generally good idea of what your needs are when looking for a dog.

So don't say that you want a dog of a certain size because you believe that it will be happy in your home.

As you read through the rest of the questions you will see that there are many other factors involved in keeping a dog happy, and size is only one aspect.

Where Will Your Dog Stay?

Before you get a dog, you will need to think to yourself, "Where will I keep the dog?" It's not enough that you have a large yard or a spacious new dog house.

As I keep mentioning, dogs are sociable animals, and leaving them outside to deal with life on their own won't go down well with most dogs. Even the toughest watchdog needs a kind word here and there to keep its sprits up and willing.

In the case of certain dogs you might find that although you have a large back garden for them to run around in, they much prefer to spend their time by your side.

This means that they will most likely be in the house more often than not. You will have to decide early on whether this is acceptable or not.

If you get an especially sociable animal then you might find that no matter how hard you try you won't be able to boot it out of the house. Somewhat reminiscent of the end scene from the "Flintstone's" cartoon where the "dog" Dino is put out of the house but finds a way back in anyway.

Regardless of this however, you will need to provide adequate space and housing for your dog. This way you know that there is somewhere for it to stay when you're not at home, or when you put the dog outside for the night (or day).

This is also a good idea if you want to train your dog from the beginning itself, to treat his own personal space as his, and not a place that he comes to only when he's annoyed at you!

Housing for your dog doesn't need to be anything fancier than your basic doghouse or even the garage or the garden shed.

As long as there is adequate space to contain the dog with no discomfort on the part of the dog, if it is weather proofed so that he doesn't get wet or snow bound, and if there is more than adequate lighting and breathing space, you (and your dog) should be fine.

Anything that comes under the heading of personalized luxury doghouses is just an added bonus. Be warned though that sometimes no matter how well appointed the doghouse is, your dog just won't stay inside.

In this case you will need to find alternate housing which is more suited to your dog. After all, if you have preferences about the way that your home should look like, and if you won't even consider living in certain places, what makes a dog any different?

Then again, depending on the breed of dog you're getting, your dog "housing" can be a dog bed or even a dog blanket. There are a number of these available to purchase these days and most promise a good night's sleep for your dog.

And if you're thinking to yourself that in earlier days dogs would have spent the night out on the porch and that should work for your dog as well, think again. Dogs these days are much the same as kids, and need more luxuries then they previously would have done without!

Do You Want an Active Dog or a Couch Potato?

You will need to decide whether you want an active energetic dog, or one who will loll around on the couch right alongside you. You will need to decide this early on as not all dogs are suited to lazing around, some of them need to be kept active for most of the day.

If on the other hand you yourself are an active person then you might find that you prefer an active dog who will fit in with your lifestyle and who can accompany you when you're out running, hiking etc.

I have mentioned this elsewhere in the book, but here it is again, you cannot judge the activity level of a dog simply by looking at its size.

A large dog needn't be either energetic or a couch potato. It can be either one of these or it can be a moderately active dog, needing only a certain amount of activity per day.

The same applies to a small dog. It can be either highly energetic or lethargic, or it can be neither. The activity level of each dog varies and depends to a very large extent on the breed of the dog and not the size.

So although you might have specified that you want a large dog in the earlier section "The Size of the Dog", you can't expect that dog to be active.

If you want a highly active dog, a moderately active dog, or even a non-active dog, you will need to specify this.

You should also know that if you do get an active dog and keep him inactive for most of his days, only going out once in a while, you will have an unhappy dog on your hands.

It is also up to you to decide what you mean by "active". Does this mean you want a dog who will bound out of bed and go for walkies whenever you want, play tennis, ball and generally frolic with you.

Or does it mean that you want a dog who will appreciate one or two instances of walkies with you per day, but no more than that.

What you really need to do therefore in this section, is to categorize how active *you* are. If you live an active life then it's a good bet that you will also want a dog that can keep up with your active lifestyle.

The same applies if you live only a moderately active lifestyle. You will then, probably prefer the faithful companion who sits uncomplainingly next to you as you watch all the latest TV programs, and wait patiently for you to finish one before having to go outside for walkies.

And remember that when you're describing your lifestyle as active, it could, and in fact probably does, differ widely from my, and other people's, opinion of what an active lifestyle is.

Be as specific as you can get. List down the activities that you like to do daily and/or weekly, this can help to outline just how active you are and how active you will want your dog to be.

Just one thing though. When you're listing these activities down, be sure and list down the ones that you're doing at the moment and have probably been doing for some time now.

Listing the ones that you would *like* to do but haven't started on as yet, is probably not the way to go about it. And if you're the king (or queen) of starting new fads you might want to list only the ones that you have kept up with, and not all the ones that you started, but stopped due to some reason or other!

Remember there is no shame in being an active couch potato. I myself am one most of the time, although I do find the time and the energy to roll off my couch and give my dogs the necessary exercise.

The Amount of Time You're Willing to Spend on Grooming

Although it has become somewhat of a fad, not too many people are willing to fork over that kind of money to have their dog groomed by professional dog groomers.

It really depends on how far you're willing to go in the matter of grooming your dog.

Some people take their dog to a professional groomer's once a year, some people once a month, others once a week, and yet others still more frequently, up to at least once a day.

As I said, this all depends on how far you're willing to go for the sake of your dog. Then again, a professional dog grooming service isn't really all that necessary if you can do the job yourself and on a regular basis.

This is also a good time for you to bond even more with your dog. If you go about it the right way, you'll find that your dog is looking forward to having a good grooming.

This question comes into play in the choosing of your dog however, not for any other reason, than because if you don't really have that much time to spare on the grooming necessities for you dog, you will have to look for a low maintenance dog where grooming isn't a top priority.

You should be able to get away with brushing your dog's coat about once a week for the really low-maintenance-grooming dogs. Your other choice is of course to use a professional grooming service if you have your heart set on a high-maintenance-grooming dog.

Whatever you decide though, you will need to do some grooming for your dog regardless of whether you do it, or you get someone else to do it for you. Grooming is an essential part of a dog's routine, and this includes bathing, cleaning their mouth, and trimming their toenails as well.

Neglecting your dog's grooming needs is something akin to if you went a whole week or two without bathing, brushing your teeth or brushing your hair.

It might look hip and cool for a few days in a grunge sort of way, but you can be assured that after that people will start avoiding you like you carry the plague, which you might very well be doing under all that dirt!

I can' tell you exactly how much time you need to spend for a day or a week on grooming your dog because each dog's requirements are different. You will need to check up on these individually for each dog breed.

What I can tell you though, is that you need to groom your dog, and you need to spend enough time on the task that you actually manage to bathe him and thoroughly brush through your dog's coat.

This will also help in the shedding-of-fur department and will keep the swirling fur-balls on your floors, down to a minimum.

What Type of Coat Would You Prefer – Long or Short?

No, I'm not asking you about next season's fashions, or even your personal preference in outdoor wear. I'm asking you what type of coat, or fur to be clearer, clearer, you would ideally like your dog to have.

This is really dependent on a number of factors chief among them being whether or not you're allergic to dog hair. (I've covered that particular topic in the last point in this section "Are you allergic to dogs".)

Regardless of this however, this is the point at which you need to decide whether you want a dog with short coat hairs which are almost non-existent, or whether you want a dog with long silken hair which will need constant grooming.

Then again, you could go the middling path and get a dog with not-too-long and not-too-short coat hairs.

If you're looking at getting a dog with short coat hairs because you believe that it won't shed as much, then think again. Some dogs shed more than others regardless of the length of their coat.

It all depends on the breed of dog you get, and has nothing to do with the coat. There's also the little matter of climate involved as well. Some dogs will shed more of their coat hairs if they are not in a suitable climate for them.

You also need to take into account the amount of grooming time that you will need to spend on your dog. If you get a dog with long hair, then almost certainly you will need to groom the dog on a frequent and regular basis.

If on the other hand you get a dog with short hair, your grooming efforts will most likely only be minimal.

You do need to take all of these into account when you're deciding on the better length of coat that you would like for your dog. However, here again you really should avoid using such ambiguous terms as long coat, short coat, or medium coat.

Everyone's idea of long and short vary, and if you're trying to tell someone that you want a large dog with a medium length coat, you're as likely to get a German Shepard as you are to get an Afghan Hound.

So try and be more specific, look through images of dogs to find out which ones have long coats and which ones have short coats.

All you really need are about three to four examples which you can cite to give the person a better idea about the length of coat you're looking for on a dog.

The Amount of Money You're Willing to Spend

There are two distinct, different types of monetary concerns that you're going to have to look into when you're considering getting a dog.

The first of these is the initial amount of money that you're going to have spend to get your dog. Unless you're getting the purebred variety of dog breed however, you won't have to spend too much in this initial stage.

That is, at least not for your dog. You will however need to have an initial outlay ready to cover the cost of doggy food, doggy bowls and a doggy bed or house.

Let's not forget the chew toy or two so that he has something to play with, and other sundry little items that will almost definitely catch your eye and which you (not the dog), must have.

That's only the first part of the initial outlay.

You will then have a secondary stage which includes such things as veterinary runs, grooming necessities, and sometimes in the event of misfortune happening and your dog running off and biting someone, third party insurance as well as other types of insurance.

And that's for starters. You will then have to calculate your monthly outgoings as needed for the dog and see if you are able to afford the costs of upkeep for him.

Even if you never get insurance or buy him another chew toy ever again, you will still need to spend on food and veterinary costs. These will be the two constants in your life and depending on the size and the breed of the dog, you will find that your costs go up or down.

For most people these are not a problem, and they will also find that they can even get the additional chew toy or two along with insurance to cover any possibilities.

But if these are beyond your means, and the chew toy becomes a treat that you get for you dog when he's been especially good, then you should only take the basics into account. Namely these are,

- Veterinary bills

- Food costs

- Grooming essentials

Monthly, this won't necessarily be such a large problem and you will find that the costs merge with your own daily and monthly costs hardly any problem.

And you really don't need to calculate these costs now anyway. What you need to do, is come to a realization that your monthly outgoings will grow slightly as you bring in another mouth to feed.

Having said that, for me, the companionship and joy that my dogs bring me are well worth the money and effort that I spend on them, and I know that I for one, will always have a dog in my life.

Do You Want to Train the Dog?

This question is necessary only to find out what sort of temperament you want in your dog. Do you want a dog that is trainable or do you want a dog that will roam wild. It all really comes down to the decision of whether you want to train your dog or not.

This is a fair question since not everyone wants to train their dog. Some people have no time or patience to go through anything other than the most rudimentary house training required, while others just don't have the inclination to go through the entire training process.

There are as usual, ways and means around this little problem and you will find that they come in the form of puppy kindergartens, and dog training classes.

Then again not everyone wants to send their dog to school to be trained. I have to say that personally I prefer to go through at least the rudimentary training process by myself, because then I find that my dog gets to know me better and this is better in the long run.

Besides, I have a soft heart and can't bear the thought of sending my dogs to someone else to train, someone who may not treat (by that I mean pamper) my dogs the way that I do.

This is not to say that these dog training schools are not good, only that I prefer not to use these services myself.

That said, if you do want to train your dog but find that you are short of the time and the patience, these doggy training schools are just what you need.

To that end, the question you want to ask yourself here is not whether you want to train the dog, but whether you want a trainable dog. Not all dogs are trainable so you will need to take that into factor when you're looking for a dog.

Is Exercising the Dog Going to be a Problem?

Not everyone likes to go out in the middle of the pouring rain to exercise their dog, but it is a fact that there are many people who would do that and more for their dogs.

I might love my dogs but I know that I'm definitely not one of those people who would brave the pouring rain for my dogs. There's nothing wrong with admitting that you want to stay home and dry.

The question that arises here however is not that of whether you would exercise your dogs in the pouring rain, but whether you want to exercise them at all.

Obviously here as well, the breed of the dog counts a lot as some dogs are more sedentary than others, and some dogs are hyper almost from the get-go.

You will also get the more moderate dogs who only require a reasonable amount of exercise, and most people find that these types of dogs suits them the best.

When the exercise question crops up however as it must, you need to decide whether you're a gung-ho exercise fanatic or whether you can live without it and be quite happy.

You will also need to look into the different needs of the dogs as well. Not all dogs are the same and each breed requires different exercise times and routines.

You could exercise a Terrier or a Spaniel for about 15 minutes, twice a day and find that your dog is satisfied, but what about if you get an Akita or a Border Collie? Two bouts of 15 minutes each day of sedentary walking is almost definitely not going to satisfy them.

And although you might have your heart set on one of these types of dogs, you need to make sure that you can cater for their need to run and frolic and generally get exercise somehow, because otherwise you will find that your dog is dissatisfied and showing signs of it in their mannerisms and lack of enthusiasm.

Is the Dog Going to be Left Alone for Most of the Day?

Another thing that you need to look into in all seriousness is whether or not your dog is going to be left alone for a large portion of the day.

Most of us need to work and this is fine as long as we take this into account when we're getting our dog.

No one can stay in the house twenty-four hours a day, and we most definitely can't always take our dogs with us everywhere that we're going.

This means that there will be times when the dog is left alone to fend for itself. You have the option of putting the dog outside during that time or leaving him inside.

If you leave your dog inside the house however, and he isn't trained, or he's still a very young puppy, or for some reason you become very late, you might find that when you get home that things are not quite as neat and tidy as when you left.

In the case of the young puppy it is mainly due to the destructive tendencies that young of all species have. That curious nature coupled with an absentee owner can lead to many an item being "explored". No stone will be left unturned in their quest to slake to their curiosity.

You will also find that very young puppies also have separation anxiety. They have after all just been weaned from their mother, their siblings, and their very familiar surroundings, and dumped willy-nilly into a stranger's house.

And to add insult to injury they have now to all intents and purposes, been abandoned. It is therefore only natural that these destructive tendencies will come to the fore.

The same applies to an untrained dog. If they are as yet not secure with your affections you will find that your house has been ransacked.

With an older dog you will find that these tendencies wane as time goes by and they become more secure in your affections. When faced with a long overdue and absentee owner however, you might find that even these dogs are displaying signs of tantrums.

What's really important here though, is for you to know how much time your dog will be left at home alone on a daily basis. Something along the lines of whether it's going to be for about 1-2 hours, or maybe about 3-4 hours.

Sometimes you might find that you need to leave your dog alone for about half a day or even more daily, if you need to go in to work and there is no one else to look after the dog.

There is no problem with all of that as long as you are candid about the length of time that you dog will need to be alone.

Not all dogs can handle being alone for any length of time, and if this is your case, then it truly is better all around for you to find a dog who won't mind the separation.

Most of the times a watchdog will be better able to handle the supposed defection, but then again, not everyone wants a watchdog.

So take into account the number of hours that you will need to leave your dog alone for a day, and add that rough number to the rest of your answers on the checklist.

Your checklist should be coming along quite nicely by now, and you should begin to have at least a rudimentary idea of what you need in a dog.

I would however, suggest that you continue through with the entire checklist as ultimately your decision on choosing a dog will only become easier.

How Much Space (Yard Space, etc.) Do You Have to Spare?

Most people think that if they have a large back garden that they are completely qualified to have a dog regardless of anything else. This is not then case.

A large yard is not, in and of itself, enough to satisfy your dog's needs. It also doesn't mean that you will be able to have a large dog.

As you can see from the previous questions on the checklist there is more to having a dog than meet's the eye, and a large yard space alone is not going to cut it.

It helps to have a large yard, and it can make your life easier to have a large yard, but don't for one minute think that all your dog worries are over because you have one. (They could just be beginning!)

What does matter here is not how large your backyard is, but more along the lines of what the activity level of your dog is, and whether he prefers indoor activities or outdoor activities.

If the dog you get prefers to spend most of his time indoors, then the large backyard that you have won't mean anything to him. If on the other hand you get a dog who prefers to be outdoors all the time, your yard, whether large of small will be eminently suitable for him.

It's not only yard space that you have to look at here, however. You will also need to see what type of space you have all around in what your dog will consider to be his habitat.

If you have a reasonably roomy house to go along with that large yard you have, then you can be assured that most dogs will be able to find solace somewhere in your home.

If on the other hand you live in a one room apartment on the twenty-sixth floor with only a small terrace for it use as an "outside", then you might encounter a problem if you get a highly energetic dog that likes frolicking outside.

To counter this, is why you need to be very specific about the type of house of apartment that you live in.

And although it doesn't need to be said, I will say it. If you live in an apartment where pets are not welcome, then either move somewhere that welcomes pets, or don't get a dog!

The number of people who believe they can keep secret the fact that they have a pet is astonishing.

What's even more astonishing is the number of people who are surprised and angry when they find that their landlord has taken action against them, and maybe even turned the dog over to animal services.

Don't let this happen. This will only cause trauma to your dog and unnecessary hassle for you.

There's no problem with finding a dog to suit your housing needs, and you can be assured that there will be dogs that adapt nicely to small spaces, just don't be fooled into thinking that these will all be small dogs.

Here, the size of the dog doesn't matter as much as the energy level of the dog matters.

If the dog is active and energetic, no matter what the size you will find that keeping it indoors no matter the size of the house or apartment, will be difficult. If you have a small apartment you might find that there are some large dogs that are suitable for this.

You will need to couple this with your preference for the size and activity level of your dog, along with other factors to find the dog breed that suits you.

Do You Have Children, Especially Young Babies or Toddlers?

Do you have children? This is an important question, not for the sake of finding out whether your kids are the ones who want the dog, but because in some instances, kids and dogs just don't mix.

This is especially true in the cases where you have children who are around toddler age. They won't understand why it's not a good thing to pull the dog's fur, tail, ears and sundry other parts.

They will also find it difficult to understand why you went and got a plaything for them which they can't really play with and which they can't bash or throw about as they would their other toys.

Your toddlers are still growing up and still learning, and if they are at the terrible two's stage where every other word that comes out of their angelic mouths is "NO!", then you can be sure that they won't listen to you when you tell them not to pull on the dog's tail etc.

The only time they will understand that "No", means "No" in the case of messing around with the dog, is when they get bitten.

And in these cases it is almost always the dog that comes off worse, because when all is said and done, the dog is after all just an animal, and the child is, well your child.

You have a choice to make in the case where you have very young children.

You can either put off getting a dog until your children are much older, or you can keep the dog outdoors for most of the time and send it to a good training school, or you can get an older dog that has been trained and is used to dealing with children.

All of these approaches work well for you if you have young children and want a dog as well, but please do remember that the dog also has its limits.

Even the friendliest dog will find that his patience is pushed to the limit when he is being constantly harassed by an unrepentant toddler who doesn't know any better.

Having got that out of the way, I can now tell you truthfully, that although I love dogs I do not believe in mixing young kids and dogs, no matter what the age, size or temperament of the dog.

It does pain me to say it, but a dog is just a dog in the end, not a human. And if a human can commit violent acts of crime thinkingly and unthinkingly, who's to say that a dog can't do the same.

Most dogs are highly intelligent beings and since we have no way of interpreting anything other than their most basic needs, we have no way of knowing the true nature of the dog.

We can make good guesses, but in the end, that's really all they are, guesses. There is no way for us to know that our saint-like dog won't suddenly turn on us, or our children, one day and bite the hand that feeds it.

This is why it's always a good idea to never leave young children unsupervised with dogs around.

No one will know who did what, first, but in the end it won't matter, the damage will already have been done in more ways than you can imagine.

This is also why I ask in the beginning whether you have young children or *babies* around. Babies are even more at risk than toddlers are because of their relative inability to defend themselves.

I don't mean to put you off getting a dog, but these are things that you must take into consideration when looking at getting a dog as a pet.

It is just negligence to ignore these questions, however unpalatable the answers might be, and you are doing not only yourself an injustice but also your children, as well as the dog.

There's also one other thing that you will want to take into account when looking at getting a dog with young children around to contend with as well. And this comes in the form of discipline.

If you get a puppy, then like as not, your toddler will have hours of fun with him. And you can rest easy in the knowledge that all is right in your world.

Except of course for the small fact that both your toddler and the puppy are of a like mindset. Both are highly curious, and both are probably prone to get into much mischief. (This will probably mean that where there is one, you will be able to find the other!)

You need to be aware of this penchant for getting into trouble that most young the world over have in abundance, as well as the fact that you will have to discipline and bring up not only your child but the dog as well at the same time.

You will have to do this for both, and it will probably try your patience sorely at times, but you must be ready to do this. And you must be ready to deal with this separately as well.

It's really no use punishing and disciplining the dog for something your child has done and vice versa. You will need to consider whether or not you can handle double the task of bringing up both your child and dog together at the same time.

However, if after going through this, you decide that a dog is alright to have, you will want to find a dog that is known to be good with children. There are dog breeds that are used as type of "nanny" dogs and these can be depended upon to a very large extent to be good with children.

When you are looking for a dog however, you will need to specify to whomever you're going to for a dog, that you have small children. They will then be better able to help you find the dog type that is suitable for you.

Do You Have Other Pets?

This can be a crucial factor in your decision off getting a dog, because sometimes adding a new dog to the mix of other older pets, be they of the dog variety or not, is not always a good idea.

If your older pet is a much adored and much pampered pet, then there's a good chance that jealousies could arise. In this case you will see more and more of human-like tendencies in them as they lose out on their number-one-pet spot, and they show it in their disgruntled behavior.

It's really a little like having a new baby when your other kids are older and have been the center of your attention for such a long time. The green monster raises its head and jealousy will abound unless the situation is handled in a timely and correct manner.

Of course if your pet is much older and more secure in your love and attention then there's a god chance that there will be no trouble. The same thing applies to a pet that has been well trained as well.

These pets will be less likely to give in to jealousy and you are bound to see less of tantrums and destructive behavior from them.

If on the other hand, your older pet is really not that old in years, you might find yourself facing an interesting time as you try to keep them apart.

These hold true no matter whether your old pet is a dog or not. What you need to look into here is which type of dog will find it easy to get along with your existing pet.

This will need to be a deciding factor when choosing your new dog, along with whether or not you're going to get a puppy or full grown dog.

In some instances a full grown dog might be easier if that dog has been fully trained. You can then have an easier time dealing with your pets and trying to find an amicable solution.

Some people however, find that getting a puppy is easier for them as they can more easily train him.

Whatever the case, you will want to make certain before you go any further that your new dog can live companionably with your old pet, and that your old pet won't encounter any problems with your new dog.

Why Do You Want a Dog?

Why *do* you want a dog? I've already posed this question in another guise in an earlier section as well. I did this with the thought in mind that if you don't really know the reason you're getting a dog, then it can come back to haunt you later on.

For instance if you're getting a dog to pacify your children, then you need to think long and hard about whether you're going to be ready to deal with the dog on a daily basis.

If you're getting the dog for your own companionship, then you need to think about what type of companionship you're looking for.

Do you want a dog to keep you company when you get home from work, when all you want to do is to sit down, relax and watch TV. Or do you want a dog to keep you company while you go jogging or shopping, or as you do your chores.

What about if you want a watchdog? Or a family pet for everyone to spoil. Maybe you just want someone to come home to, and whom you know you can trust to be faithful to you.

These are all valid reasons to get a dog and none are better or worse than the other one. Why you need to know this, is simply because it makes the choosing of your dog much easier.

This knowledge ties in quite nicely with the question about exercising your dog, and is asked for much the same reason.

I have said it before but I will say it again here nevertheless. A dog is a social animal, and in fact through the centuries it has been bred to become man's best friend.

To make your dog your best friend, you should really know why you want the dog in the first place. This way you won't mistakenly get a highly energetic dog when all you want is a faithful and loyal couch potato to sit right alongside you as take a break from your hard day.

Then again, there is also the fact that some dogs simply do not make good companion dogs. They are too highly strung, or they are more inclined to be working dogs, or watchdogs.

If what you want is a gentle companion to while away those lonely hours and with whom you can have a good tussle over a tennis ball with, then you probably don't want something like a Bulldog or a Mastiff.

Have You Ever Owned a Dog Before?

This particular point only helps insofar, that if you have had a dog before this, you will have a better understanding of your needs and will be able to judge to a certain extent what you're looking for in a dog more easily.

This entire thing is of course a moot point if what you want is a dog like that of your previous dog, or the dog that you already have.

If however, you're looking at getting a different breed of dog altogether from the one that have, or had, you will still find this checklist to be helpful to you.

You might want another dog, but that doesn't necessarily mean that you know exactly what type of dog you want, or that you know which type of dog would suit you best.

If your older dog is still with you and you're looking at getting a second, or third, dog I have covered this eventuality too in one of the previous sections, "Do your have other pets".

The whole point of determining whether you have had a dog is to help you in finding the right dog for you.

The first thing that you need to do is to decide whether or not you want the same breed of dog. If you don't want the same breed of dog, then do you want the same general traits and characteristics for your new dog as for the earlier dog?

What about the other things that I mention in the checklist, like size, length of coat etc. These things apply to you as well and you will want to evaluate all of these things for yourself before you get a dog.

And because you already know what it is to have a dog, and what are the perils and the pitfalls, you will find that you are better able to answer the questions.

Are You Looking for Special Traits and Characteristics?

When you think of having a dog, are you thinking about anything special? Do you want your dog to be an eternally happy dog, or would you rather have the soulful looks of a Basset Hound to contend with.

Do you want a dog who is easy to live with, or do you want a dog that will protect you and your property zealously.

What about children, do you want a dog that is good with children? Or maybe you want your faithful hound to sit beside you in the lonely hours of the night.

You might find that you want a dog to accompany you as you go about your daily activities, or you might want one that will give you a run for your money as you go jogging through the parks.

Do you want a dog to play catch and Frisbee with? Maybe a dog you can show off to your friends and neighbors, or maybe even a dog whom you can spoil and pamper and call, "my snookems"!

Whatever you want, and by now you probably get the gist of what I'm getting at, there will almost always be a dog to suit your needs and your peculiarities, and I say in this with all good intents.

And don't worry if the dog you want doesn't have all your peculiarities and idiosyncrasies yet. By the time the both of you get along like a house on fire, you will find that your dog has acquired just about all of your quirks and eccentricities, down pat.

What I'm really trying to say however, is that if you are thinking of getting a dog, then you must have some image of a sorts in your mind as to what you will do with your dog. Even if it is only to have someone to come home to after a long hard day's work.

Although all of these ideas that you have on what you can do when you have a dog are not necessarily practical or even probable, some of them are reality.

It is these ideas that you want to translate into solid plans, and it's these ideas which will help you to get a better understanding of what you're looking for in a dog.

And if you're more of a dreamer like me, and have one grand scheme after another, there will be many things that you want to do with your dog by your side, but in reality you either don't get to them, or they're not practical.

I remember that when I first got Catcher (my first dog in case you didn't remember), I wanted to go exploring around the many hills and dales that surrounded our farmhouse, and do all manner of Lassie-esque things.

Unfortunately for my rather grandiose plans, we lived not in a farmhouse, but in a two bedroom flat for most of my childhood, and as for the hills and the dales which I wanted to explore, they were for the most part not hills and dales at all, but old office buildings and apartment complexes.

Needless to say, I did not get to go exploring too much through these with my bosom companion Catcher, at my side!

It's these dreams however, that can be translated into reality, and it's these ones that you need to think about when you're going through this checklist, and this question in particular.

True, you do need to be practical, but sometimes, it helps to dream. And if in dreaming you find that you have managed to find the perfect dog for you, then all the better.

Where Do You Live
Climate-wise?

This is an important question if you're planning on getting a dog. Some dogs are highly unsuited for some temperaments and really should not be transplanted to a radically different climate.

Something like an Alaskan Husky for instance will find it very difficult to live somewhere near the equator in tropical and hot climes. Likewise a dog that is born and bred for high temperatures will find it very difficult to live in countries where there is snowfall.

So if you're looking for an ideal doggy companion for you and it looks like you might have to move soon or in the near future, or you're one of those people who have wanderlust and regularly pull up roots to go where the mood takes you, then I would suggest getting a dog that can easily acclimatize and who will be more suited to where you will be.

Obviously you can't always tell where you will be in the future. If you could do that you could make yourself a small fortune. Unfortunately, we're none of us fortune tellers and can't predict the future, so we don't know for certain where we will be in two or even ten years time.

That shouldn't prevent you from getting a dog however. If your plans now are to stay where you are, and if you won't be transplanting your dog from one temperature extreme to another, then you will have no problems.

Purebred Dog, Mixed Breed Dog or a Normal Dog?

This question is a little bit more difficult to get an answer to, because not everyone will know the difference between a Purebred dog, and a hybrid, or mixed breed dog.

The one thing that you should know about purebred dogs is that they can cost somewhere upwards of the range of $100.

If all you want is a normal dog, then you have no further to look than your local pet store or animal shelter.

In these places you will find that you have a number of options available to you on which dogs you want, and they will generally be for a reasonable price as well.

If, however, you want a purebred dog, you will need to go elsewhere other than the pet store to find your dog. Purebred dogs can normally be found only at other breeders' and places that specialize in breeding these types of dogs.

If you're looking for a purebred and you're paying those prices, you will also want to make sure that the breeder is able to give you the necessary information about these dogs.

Some people who breed these types of dogs do not necessarily have all of these answers with them. These are not your professional dog breeders with the necessary information on them, but they are for the most part instead, enthusiastic dog lovers who breed their own purebred dogs.

So what is a purebred dog, what's the difference between a purebred and hybrid dog, and most of all, why would you want a purebred dog?

Personally speaking I found these to be pressing questions indeed the first time I learned about purebred dogs, so I thought that you too might have these burning questions.

I have given you the answers to the best of my knowledge and hope that they can help you. I realize that it does not, strictly speaking, pertain to the various matters on the checklist, but it does give you a general idea about what you're looking for in this particular point.

Of course, it makes sense to realize that if you were looking for a purebred dog over a normal dog that you would already know what the difference is. This small portion therefore I dedicate to those of you who have no idea whatsoever about purebred dogs and their virtues.

A purebred dog is simply a dog which has been bred down through many generations from the same strain or breed of dog. Purebred dogs are also considered to be pedigreed dogs.

A true purebred dog breeder should be able to display the necessary lineage details of the dog. The dogs which are used for breeding purposes also need to be of a recognized variety of purebred dogs as well, for a puppy to be considered a purebred dog.

A mixed breed dog on the other hand is a dog that has been bred from two different types of purebred dogs. These are also called hybrid dogs, and they are different from your normal run of the mill mixed breed dogs that can be found on any street corner.

However, with mixed breed dogs you will find that some breeders don't always use a purebred dog to purebred dog mix. They will instead use a purebred to hybrid dog mix, which will make the resulting puppy one very confused dog indeed!

Unlike the purebred dogs whose racial traits and characteristics you can obtain easily enough, a mixed breed dog will naturally enough have a mixed set of traits and characteristics which will sometimes manifest itself in surprising ways!

If you're in interested in either a purebred dog, or a mixed breed dog, you should be able to get the history and any other relevant information from the breeders themselves.

But if what you want is the characteristics of a dog, I'm afraid that in the case of the mixed breed dogs that you will have to go hunting through the different dog varieties to find what some of their better known traits are, and then wait and see which ones manifest themselves.

Let me end this by saying that someone would normally go looking for a purebred dog for one of a few reasons. Chief among these being that they want a dog in whom the genetic traits of diseases has been all but bred out, at least to a very great extent.

Most of the purebred dogs won't succumb as easily to any of the genetic illnesses that a normal dog would succumb to over the course of time.

And for many people this is the ideal as they will be able to enjoy the friendship of their dog for longer years, without the fear that disease will take the dog away from them prematurely.

The Cuteness Factor

This is of course the all important question for many people. How cute do you want your dog to be. On a scale of one to ten, with ten being the cutest, what would your answer be?

This can become a problem because to the best of my knowledge just about all puppies are "cute", it's only when they grow into mature dogs that the problems arise and the cuteness factor goes away. (This is about the time when your kids will also start to grow weary of their dogs, so parents take note.)

If your puppy was bought mainly for the cuteness factor and you want it to continue for some years yet, then you need to do some serious homework.

You will need to look at different pictures of the different dog varieties when they are fully grown to find which dog breeds continue the cuteness factor into their lives.

For the most part though, cuteness, like any other non-definitive vague term, is relative.

Some people think that a Chihuahua and a Doberman Pinscher is cute. I personally don't see this although I usually refrain from saying this straight to the owner's face. (That I fear would just be too cruel!)

I find that I personally prefer the likes of a Labrador or a German Shepard in the puppy cuteness stakes. And even as they grow older, although they might not be cute in the traditional sense, I find that they have more of the traits that I look for in a dog.

There's no need to worry though, you won't have to go trawling through mug shot after mug shot of cute doggy pictures. Since there is somewhat of a standard of what cute is, you need only to go through the better known dog breed variety pictures to get an idea.

Or if you or your kids have already seen what is a very cute and adorable bundle of puppy, you can easily go through and find out what that puppy will look like as a full grown mature dog.

Are You Allergic to Dogs?

This might seem like a silly question to ask of someone who is thinking of getting a dog, but believe me it's not. The number of people I have come across who are allergic to their own pets is simply staggering.

There is however, a loophole here which many of these dog lovers utilize to be able to overcome their shortcomings, so if you are allergic to dog hair, which is really what people mean by being allergic to dogs, there is nothing for you to worry about, you can still get a dog as a pet.

You might need to make some sacrifices in some of your preferences of dog, but be assured that there are dogs out there for you as well.

These are known for the most part as low allergy dogs, and if you do have an allergy problem you can ask around for dog breed varieties that are suitable for allergy sufferers.

I know I was curious on hearing about these certain types of dog breeds which dog allergy sufferers could own, so at a guess you are too. Well, the secret lies not in the breed of the dog as you might be led to believe, but in the coat of the dog.

It's not the length of the coat or the thickness or even the color of the coat that matters here however. It is, very simply, how often and how much of the coat is shed by the dog at various times.

For instance, if the dog has a very short almost non-existent coat but sheds almost daily, then your average dog allergy sufferer is, well, going to suffer. So it's not the length of the coat or any other factor about the dog's coat which matters, it's how often said coat is shed.

A friend of mine – not an allergy sufferer – had a cute Japanese Spitz, and to the best of my knowledge there was never a time in the house when there wasn't dog hair strewn about the house, and this despite many attempts at controlling this problem as well.

So if you do suffer from a dog allergy, but you still love the adorable mutts, you have nothing to worry about. There is a dog out there for you who doesn't shed all over you and your house.

And if you do finally decide to get a dog that is low on the allergy scale, you might want to consider regularly using a professional grooming service. This can cut down even more on the chances of your becoming further allergic to your faithful companion.

Different Dog Breeds

In this section I have included a very few of the many hundreds of varieties of dog breeds available.

This is for a two fold reason. The first is because if I were to try and include all of the known breeds in this book, I would still be writing about them even now, there are so many of them.

And the second reason I have included this section is so that you can get a general idea of what I am talking about in the book, and what you should look for and what you will find when choosing a dog.

It should also be noted that I have for the most part included dogs in this section that are considered to be the more popular variety.

There are a handful of dog breeds here which are not as well known as, say a Husky, or a Doberman Pinscher, or a Poodle, or even a Dalmatian, but these are only a few cases.

I put them in mainly because although they might not be universally known by name, by sight they are familiar to dog lovers everywhere.

Each of the dogs I have mentioned are in alphabetical order so as to make life easier for you, and I have included the relevant details needed, to find out what you can about the dogs.

Naturally this won't be enough information for a great many people, and for these people, I direct you to use the resources which are available to you in the form of the internet, books and other such places.

For color pictures of any dog breed listed here, you can search online or check my other book, *Dog Breeds Pictures*, containing the largest collection of dog pictures available (over 100 dog breeds).

Afghan Hound

Height & Weight (male dog): 68-73 cm & 58-64 lbs.

Height & Weight (female dog): 65-70 cm; & 56-63 lbs.

Temperament: Affectionate, sweet, and loyal. These dogs can be somewhat sensitive and appear to be aloof. They need a lot of attention otherwise they are prone to pining. Better suited to people who have older children. They can also be difficult to housebreak.

Energy levels: Relatively active, and they prefer being outdoors.

Exercise: They need a minimum of about 30-40 minutes of energetic exercise which can be in the form of a good gallop.

Grooming: Should be bathed regularly about once a week. Brushing should be accomplished only after bathing the dog, as brushing a dry coat can lead to damage. These dogs can also be show dogs, in which case the grooming needs will be more extensive.

Bred as: Show dogs, are considered to be sight hounds, and are good in hunting, tracking and herding as well as being a watchdog.

Alaskan Husky

Height & Weight (male dog): 58-65 cm & 46-50 lbs.

Height & Weight (female dog): 56-61 cm; & 38-42 lbs.

Temperament: These dogs are sociable, and playful, as well as being mischievous, intelligent and trainable. They can also be difficult to housebreak, and prefer to have company. They should ideally have another companion to keep company with.

They should be kept in cold climates, or if in hot temperatures, in the cold of a shade or air conditioning. Not suitable as guard dogs as they are very friendly.

Energy levels: Very active

Exercise: They need a fair amount of exercise to keep them happy and healthy, but be certain that this is not done in the excessive heat.

Grooming: Doesn't shed much, mainly there only during the two shedding seasons. In these seasons their coats need to be brushed with a steel comb to get all the shedding fur out.

Bred as: Working Dogs

Alaskan Malamute

Height & Weight (male dog): 61-66 cm & 80-95 lbs.

Height & Weight (female dog): 56-61 cm & 70-85 lbs.

Temperament: Affectionate and playful, loyal, sociable and intelligent. They are not suitable as guard dogs as they are very friendly. They also need and love a lot of attention. Until they become very mature, these dogs can be resemble rambunctious puppies, and they make great companions.

Energy levels: Fairly active, with high energy levels. These are not suitable apartment dogs.

Exercise: Needs much exercise and is best pleased when running around. They should not be exercised excessively however as they are more suited for cooler climes.

Grooming: Sheds quite a lot, and needs to be groomed at least twice a week.

Bred as: Working Dogs, they love to pull sleds

Basset Hound

Height & Weight (male dog): 30-38 cm & 59-65 lbs.

Height & Weight (female dog): 28-36 cm & 45-60 lbs

Temperament: These dogs are peaceful and gentle, and make devoted friends. They make great family dogs, and are friendly with children. They have a mild nature, and can perform tricks. Housebreaking these dogs is not always easy and will require time and patience.

Energy levels: Relatively active. They are more active outdoors than inside, but they will be able to live indoors without a problem.

Exercise: They need plenty of exercise and if you take it outside, this dog will run around for hours.

Grooming: They shed constantly, but you only need to groom them when the need arises. Toenails will need to be trimmed regularly, and you will need to clean behind the cars regularly as well because of the large drooping size of them.

Bred as: Hound Dogs (as the name suggests!) they are used for hunting purposes as well.

Beagle

Height & Weight (male dog): 36-41cm & 22-25 lbs

Height & Weight (female dog): 33-38 cm & 20-23lbs

Temperament: Very friendly and intelligent. Known to be sociable, and excellent with children. They don't like to be left alone, and would be better off as one of a pair. They also have a loud baying-type of howl that can be surprising if you've never heard it before. Some people find it to be disturbing, so you will need to consider the neighbors' reactions as well.

Energy levels: Very active, especially indoors and make great apartment pets. A small yard should suffice.

Exercise: They need plenty of exercise, but if you have a yard they can roam around, this should be catered for. They will like to have daily brisk walks though.

Grooming: Shedding is average, and they need to be groomed only once in a while.

Bred as: Hound dog

Border Collie

Height & Weight (male dog): 48-56 cm & 30-45 lbs

Height & Weight (female dog): 46-53 cm & 27-42 lbs

Temperament: Obedient, intelligent and are trainable. They are also sensitive, and have been found in some cases to be good with children. However, they can also be aggressive with children depending on what the dog is doing at the time. They also tend to pine and/ or become neurotic if left alone for long periods of time.

Energy levels: They are highly active, energetic dogs and are not recommended as apartment dogs.

Exercise: You will need to exercise these dogs and then some. They love to work as this is what they were born and bred for, and you will find that they do very well in dog sports.

Grooming: An average shedder, you will nevertheless need to brush the coat regularly to keep it in a shiny and gleaming condition. Bathing should only be done when necessary.

Bred as: Working Dogs

Bulldog

Height & Weight (male dog): 31-40 cm & 53-55 lbs

Height & Weight (female dog): 31-40 cm & 49-51 lbs

Temperament: This dog is known to be gentle and good with children. Its intimidating appearance will put many people off, but it is a very intelligent dog. It makes and excellent guard dog, and loves to be with people. They love all the attention that they can get, although they do tend to drool a lot.

Energy levels: Mostly they are an inactive breed, and do well indoors.

Exercise: They need regular exercise, although some would prefer not have any exercise at all. This depends to a large extent on the dog itself however, as some dogs love the exercise.

Grooming: Average shedder, and needs grooming only when necessary.

Bred as: Working Dogs

Chihuahua

Height & Weight (male dog): 30-38 cm & 59-65 lbs

Height & Weight (female dog): 30-38 cm & 59-65 lbs

Temperament: This tiny dog has an inimitable source of love and affection for their owners, but they are not good pets to have with children around. They are energetic, and loyal, and can be swift as well.

They are also intelligent and willing to learn what you set them, but you might need some patience to accomplish this as some of them can be willful.

Energy levels: These dogs are relatively active, although they make great apartment dogs.

Exercise: Regular exercise is needed, although walks will probably best suit it.

Grooming: Average shedder. Needs to be brushed regularly to keep the coat gleaming.

Bred as: Toy dogs

Cocker Spaniel

Height & Weight (male dog): 35-38 cm & 15-30 lbs

Height & Weight (female dog): 34-36 cm & 7-15 lbs

Temperament: Gentle and sweet, this dog is very loyal and happy. They can be difficult to housebreak, but on the up-side they are good with children and love to be with people. They need lots of affection and give lots of affection back to everyone around them.

Energy levels: They are a fairly active breed and also do well indoors.

Exercise: They need to be exercised regularly, and love to go on walks.

Grooming: An average shedder, regular brushing is needed to look after the long silky coat.

Bred as: Gun/ Hunting Dogs

Dachshund

Height & Weight (male dog): 35-45 cm & 18-20 lbs

Height & Weight (female dog): 35-45 cm & 16-19 lbs

Temperament: Intelligent and loyal, this dog can also be willful and at times playful. They can become jealous of other pets if not brought up to be sociable from an early age, and they can also be obstinate.

Energy levels: Fairly active

Exercise: They need regular exercise and a bout of playing doesn't go amiss either.

Grooming: Average shedder, needs only regular grooming.

Bred as: Hound dogs, used for hunting.

Dalmatian

Height & Weight (male dog): 50-60cm & 53-58 lbs

Height & Weight (female dog): 50-55 cm & 50-55 lbs

Temperament: Friendly and playful, they are great companions and make life interesting. They are good with older children as they are often very playful themselves whatever their age.

They need attention and affection, and thrive on good treatment. They are also a fastidious and clean breed. Very reliable they can be found at the heels of their master more often than not.

Energy levels: Very active, needs space to run about.

Exercise: They are extremely active dogs and love to run and play. They love to have daily walks and will be extremely willing to go out at any time.

Grooming: Constant shedding, although there are two major shedding seasons a year. They need continued grooming to deal with this.

Bred as: Companion and show Dogs

English Shepard

Height & Weight (male dog): 46-58 cm & 45-60 lbs

Height & Weight (female dog): 46-58 cm & 40-50 lbs

Temperament: They make great guard dogs, and are very intelligent. They are also loyal and courageous. These dogs are also good with children and love to interact with family members. They can be wary of strangers however, which is why they make good guard dogs.

Energy levels: Very active. They can be kept as apartment dogs, but they need a lot of exercise and activity to keep them happy.

Exercise: Regular and frequent exercise is what's needed with these dogs.

Grooming: Average shedder. They will only need to be groomed regularly.

Bred as: Working Dogs

Foxhound

Height & Weight (male dog): 53-64 cm & 65-75 lbs

Height & Weight (female dog): 50-63 cm & 63-75 lbs

Temperament: These dogs make great pets for children, and they are known to be loving and affectionate. They are playful and active, and can in some instances be difficult to housebreak.

Energy levels: Very active, and not suited as an apartment dog.

Exercise: Needs lots of exercise so unless you have a very large for it run around in, or you plan to give it regular strenuous exercise and play, don't get this dog.

Grooming: Average shedder, needs to be brushed regularly to keep the coat shiny and healthy.

Bred as: Hound dog

German Shepard

Height & Weight (male dog): 60-65 cm & 77-85 lbs

Height & Weight (female dog): 55-60 cm & 75-85 lbs

Temperament: Very intelligent, and they make very good guard dogs. They are great companions and loyal to their masters. They are known to be fearless and will follow directions you give quiet cheerfully.

They need much attention and don't like to be left alone. If they are trained properly they can be very good with children, but only if they are trained properly. Otherwise they can grow up to be protective and aggressive.

Energy levels: Very active, they don't make good apartment dogs although they can adapt.

Exercise: They need to be exercised and love to have a lot of play and activity to keep them busy.

Grooming: Constant shedder. Brushing should be done on a fairly regular basis, while bathing needs to be kept to a minimum.

Bred as: Herd dogs, watchdogs

Golden Retriever

Height & Weight (male dog): 56-61 cm & 60-80 lbs

Height & Weight (female dog): 51-56 cm & 55-70 lbs

Temperament: Intelligent, loving and lovable, well trained dogs will also have beautiful manners. They make great companion and family dogs and are known to be good with children as well. They are loyal and are also good as watchdogs as they are not overly friendly with strangers.

Energy levels: Relatively active, these dogs will normally do well as apartment dogs.

Exercise: Regular daily exercise is the key here, although they like to play a lot, so this can be another form of exercise if maintained for a sufficient amount of time.

Grooming: Average shedder, needs grooming regularly. Bathe infrequently, but you can use a dry shampoo more frequently.

Bred as: Working Dogs, competition dogs, and also used as dogs for the blind or disabled.

Japanese Sptiz

Height & Weight (male dog): 30-38 cm & 11-20 lbs

Height & Weight (female dog): 30-38 cm & 11-20 lbs

Temperament: These dogs make excellent companion dogs although they can have destructive tendencies if left alone for too long. They are mischievous and energetic and love nothing more than to spend their time playing.

They are intelligent and make good watchdogs. They are very loyal and affectionate towards the people they know, and are wary of strangers. They are also in some instances very territorial if they are not socialized at a young age.

Energy levels: Fairly active, but they are good apartment dogs.

Exercise: They need plenty of exercise to keep their playful natures happy, and a reasonable sized yard will cover most of these requirements. Long walks (on a leash) will also be appreciated as these dogs love to prance about.

Grooming: Average shedder, but if in the wrong climate, this dog can become a constant shedder. The long hair needs to combed on a regular basis, and should be combed with a mind to the thick under layer of fur as well.

Bred as: Companion Dogs

Lakeland Terrier

Height & Weight (male dog): 30-36cm & 15-17 lbs

Height & Weight (female dog): 30-36 cm & 13-15 lbs

Temperament: Affectionate, intelligent this dog also has a wandering attention span and sometimes needs to be recalled to its training with a firm hand. They are very lovable however, and make faithful companions. They are known to be feisty and playful, and loves to play with children as well.

Energy levels: Relatively active, they make good apartment dogs, and don't even need a yard.

Exercise: They love to play and need to be exercised regularly.

Grooming: Sheds very little. The old hair needs to be either combed out, or plucked out by hand. Dogs used as show dogs, will need a more extensive grooming schedule, otherwise they can have infrequent grooming.

Bred as: Companion and show dog, also a hunting dog

Mastiff

Height & Weight (male dog): upwards of: 76 cm & 160 lbs

Height & Weight (female dog): upwards of: 69 cm & 150 lbs

Temperament: These dogs are known to be calm and docile, and they are generally good tempered. They can be good with children, but not with overly young children or babies due to the large size of the dogs. They also make good guard dogs.

Energy levels: Relatively inactive, they need to be exercised well if they are to be kept in an apartment.

Exercise: Regular exercise is needed to keep these dog fit. You might have to force the issue as they are not inclined to be happy about exercise.

Grooming: Average shedder

Bred as: Working Dogs

Newfoundland

Height & Weight (male dog): 69-74 cm & 130-150 lbs

Height & Weight (female dog): 63-69 cm & 100-120 lbs

Temperament: Has a good and even temperament and is one of the breeds best known to be good with children. They are intelligent and loving, and make excellent companion dogs.

They are very loyal and will react if their master or family is threatened in any way. These dogs are also more suited to cooler climates, so you need to be careful when keeping them in hot climes.

Energy levels: Relatively active, they can make good apartment dogs if exercised properly.

Exercise: They need regular exercise, although exercising it in hot weather can be dangerous for it. This a great dog to go swimming with and you will find that it likes to play.

Grooming: Average shedder, with two shedding seasons. The coat of this dog will benefit from twice weekly or weekly brushing.

Bred as: Working Dogs

Pomeranian

Height & Weight (male dog): 18-30cm & 3-7 lbs

Height & Weight (female dog): 18-30 cm & 3-7 lbs

Temperament: They are intelligent little dogs who also make good watchdogs. They will be wary of any strangers who enter their territory and if trained properly can warn you if there is someone at the door.

They are also known to be temperamental dogs, and can at times be willful. This can make it harder to train these dogs, but patience and a firm go a long way to helping in this. They need constant love and care and like to know that they are the center of attention.

Energy levels: Very active, but indoors. They will make good apartment dogs.

Exercise: They are very playful dogs and love the exercise to be had from that. They also love to walk and will gladly go for long walks with you.

Grooming: Constant shedder, although there are two shedding seasons. The coat needs to be brushed regularly to keep it from becoming entangled and gnarled.

Bred as: Toy Dogs

Poodle (Standard)

Height & Weight (male dog): upwards of 38 cm & 47-50 lbs

Height & Weight (female dog): upwards of 38 cm & 45-60 lbs

Temperament: They make great companion dogs and are very good-natured and pleasant to have around. They can be sensitive, but they are intelligent and very loyal. They have calm and sensible dispositions and this tends to show through in their dignified mannerisms.

Energy levels: Relatively inactive, they make great apartment dogs.

Exercise: These dogs aren't fond of excessive exercise although they do like to run about and play. One thing that they seem to like however, is swimming, so these dogs make excellent companions in the water.

Grooming: Sheds very little, and is known as a good dog for dog-allergy sufferers. Much grooming is needed to keep this dog in top condition, and this includes regular almost daily brushing of the coat.

Bred as: Companion and show dogs, also known to be gun dogs as well as sporting dogs.

Ridgeback

Height & Weight (male dog): 63-69 cm & 80-90 lbs

Height & Weight (female dog): 61-66 cm & 65-75 lbs

Temperament: Although some say that this is a good dog with children, they can be of an uncertain temperament, and might not deal too well with the innocent roughhousing of young children.

These dogs are however, gentle and are very obedient. Good natured while they are at home, when they are on the hunt they can be ferocious and awesome to behold. They are very loyal and will walk through fire for a good owner.

Energy levels: Very active, with lots of stamina. They are however, relatively inactive when indoors. These dogs are not suitable for small apartments, although they can adapt.

Exercise: They need lots of exercise and a large yard is always ideal. Anything strenuous in the way of exercise and play will do, and they are quite happy to keep on going, long after you think they would be tired out.

Grooming: An average shedder, this dog will benefit from regular grooming.

Bred as: Hound dogs, hunting dogs

Rottweiler

Height & Weight (male dog): 61-69 cm & 95-130 lbs

Height & Weight (female dog): 56-63 cm & 85-115 lbs

Temperament: This dog is known to be immensely trainable and has a calm temperament. They are also very ferocious and although they are also very obedient, they do not mix as well with children. If they are trained properly they will be very social although they do need a lot in the way of companionship.

Energy levels: Great stamina, and mainly inactive if kept indoors. A large yard is preferable.

Exercise: You will find that this dog has a great stamina and positively loves to exercise. Swimming is something they love to do, and you will find that they also love to play with you.

Grooming: Average shedder, but needs to be groomed regularly to keep the coat glossy.

Bred as: Working Dogs

Tibetan Terrier

Height & Weight (male dog): 36-43 cm & 18-30 lbs

Height & Weight (female dog): 36-43 cm & 18-30 lbs

Temperament: These dogs are wary of strangers, and loyal to their masters. They are playful and can be very mischievous at times. They have an even temperament although they can be snappish if they are constantly bothered. This is why they do better with older children than with younger children.

Energy levels: Active, but can be kept in an apartment type setting if exercised regularly.

Exercise: This dog is very active and should be given the opportunity to exercise it all out. Running is a good option, and if you have a yard, they should manage to get what exercise they need, although additional walks are also appreciated.

Grooming: Sheds very little and is known to be good for dog-allergy sufferers if the coat is kept well groomed. This dog does however, require an extensive grooming regimen and needs to have its coat brushed at least twice to three times a week to prevent tangling.

Excess under-hairs also need to be removed otherwise there can be some shedding. Bathing is also required very frequently.

Bred as: Herd dogs

Welsh Corgi

Height & Weight (male dog): 25-30 cm & 25-30 lbs

Height & Weight (female dog): 25-30 cm & 24-28 lbs

Temperament: Intelligent, obedient and devoted. What more could you ask for in man's best friend? They are also known to be protective, although this can become territorial if not trained out of them from an early age through socialization. They are also known to interact well with children.

Energy levels: Active. They are most active indoors and are fine as apartment dogs.

Exercise: Since they are so active, exercise is necessary for them to keep them fit, but not strenuous exercise.

Grooming: Shedding occurs mainly twice a year. Regular brushing of the short coat will keep it glossy and healthy.

Bred as: Herd dogs

Yorkshire Terrier

Height & Weight (male dog): 15-17 cm & 6-7lbs

Height & Weight (female dog): 15-17 cm & 6-7 lbs

Temperament: These dogs are known as little warriors and have a heart of gold. They are highly intelligent and loyal to their masters. Not particularly good with young children they are nevertheless good little dogs. They need a lot of attention and are territorial.

Energy levels: Not very active out of doors, this dog is nevertheless quite active when indoors. This makes it eminently suitable for apartment living.

Exercise: they will benefit from small amounts of daily exercise, although they do love to play.

Grooming: Sheds very little, and is suitable for allergy sufferers. Regular grooming is required however to keep their coats clean and tangle free.

Show dogs require an extensive grooming schedule to keep their coats in top condition. These dogs also need to have their teeth cleaned regularly to prevent tooth decay and infection.

Bred as: Show dogs, and Toy dogs

Your Resources

This section I thought I would use to list some of the possible resources which are available to you in your quest to find your perfect canine companion.

Naturally there will more resources available to you than those that I have listed here, but these are the more popular methods available so far.

Pet Stores

These are the most obvious places for you to look to find your dog, unless of course you want a purebred dog. In that case, a pet store isn't necessarily the place that you want to look.

Having said that, with the exception of these specially bred dogs, you will find that most of your doggy needs can be met from the pet store.

Not only will you be able to find the dog f your choice, but you will also be able to find all the necessary (and unnecessary) accoutrements for your dog.

In fact pet stores are probably your best bet if you don't have a particular breed of dog in mind. With your checklist in hand you will have a better idea of the type of dog you want, and the personnel at these pet stores will be able to help you narrow your search down even more.

But, just like I mentioned earlier, if you're going more to investigate your options than to make an actual purchase, then may I reiterate on what I said earlier, and suggest again that you leave your wallet at home?

Otherwise you can be sure that you will end up coming back home with a dog you had no intention of getting!

A pet store is also, if memory serves me, one of the better places for kids to get their first dog from.

It serves many purposes to do this, but the best reason is that you will then be able to give your kids an almost-free reign of the pet store to choose their dog.

You will of course have some idea of what you want having first gone through the checklist, but that just makes it all the more easier to gently nudge your kids in the direction you want with a little help from the pet store personnel!

Of course you should get to pet store people before your kids get to thee dogs, otherwise you might still end up with a dog that you don't want when they go around and see the many adorable puppy faces!

Animal Shelters

This is where I found my eight year old Lab, and this I am afraid to say where most unwanted dogs, or homeless and lost dogs will end up.

You will find puppies at these shelters but for the most part there will be more older dogs to be found here. If you're thinking about getting a dog from one of these places you will want to first determine whether you want an older dog or not.

And if you are getting an older dog, you will need to make sure that bad training habits have not made the dog unable to live with in easy companionship.

Most of these dogs also come from traumatic experiences so you will need to be aware that they might display behaviors that they otherwise normally wouldn't.

These can include timidity, fear when you come near the dog, and sometimes even an adverse reaction to something that triggers a flashback to a bad event.

Online Help

These days there is extensive online help available for you to find and keep a dog in the way that it should be maintained.

There are many sites which you can use to help you go through and find the dog f your choice, and there are many sites dedicated to helping you keep your dog happy.

It's simply a matter of finding these sites and finding the information that interests you.

You will be able to find places that you give you information the various types of dogs, their needs, dog shows and competitions and even sites giving you detailed information on your dog.

You will be able to find such things as kennel clubs and information on where you can find one near you.

There will be forums which you can join to have discussions with like minded people who love their dogs just as much as you do, and you will also be able to find online stores which sells doggy needs, (like that lovely squishy rubber ducky chew toy which you just know your dog would love!).

However, you should also be wary of sites which just want to draw in people to make money. This being the age of the internet, scams also abound on the internet, which seem genuine enough at first glance.

So what are these places and how do you get there? The simple answer is for you to log on to the internet and go through a search engine to find what you need.

But this can be time consuming in the extreme, so to circumvent that I have included the names of a few places that you might find useful.

And if you want more than the ones that I have given you below, you can always ask your dog loving friends how they go about the whole thing.

- American Kennel Club – www.akc.org

- Canadian Kennel Club – www.ckc.ca/en/

- The Kennel Club (UK) – www.kennelclub.org.uk

- Australian National Kennel Council – www.ankc.aust.com

- Dog Domain, for everything dog – www.dogdomain.com

- Federation Cynologique Internationale – www.fci.be

Now You Have Your Dog

This section is dedicated for what you need to do after you get your dog, although it can be a good idea to look through this to get a general idea of what needs doing even before you get your dog.

Most of these subjects I have touched upon in the earlier sections, some of them in great detail others only lightly, but I will go through them again, and this time you will find that you are looking at them with a different mindset.

At this point I am assuming that you have chosen (and maybe even gotten) your dog. I now concentrate on a few of the things that you need to do to take good care of your dog.

The items that I have listed here are only a very few with good reason. Most dogs require different routines and different factors to keep them happy.

The ones I have gone through here are the most basic of requirements, so don't be surprised to find a few missing from the list that you might normally do.

For instance I have not mentioned doggy insurance here as this is a very personal thing and changes from country to country as well as insurance company to insurance company.

You might ask "don't veterinarians fall into the same category?" and don't they also change accordingly, but there is a vast difference here.

Every dog needs a veterinarian, and will for the most part receive the care and attention of one besides which all veterinarians are there for the purpose of caring for animals. Not everyone will look to get doggy insurance however, and not everyone feels that this type of insurance is necessary.

Once you get your dog you will find that most of these requirements that I have mentioned below, in fact probably all of these, apply to you and your dog.

Having had a dog as my companion for most of my life, I can say that I have been through most of the ups and downs to be found in a shared doggy life, and therefore feel fully qualified to comment on these aspects on what a dog's very basic needs will be.

The topics I have covered in this section are,

- The Veterinarian

- Feeding your dog

- Giving your dog affection

- Grooming your dog

- Leaving your dog alone for any length of time

- And the fact that really, every dog *is* different

Veterinary Runs

If you truly care about yourself and your dog, you will find a good veterinarian for your dog as soon as possible. Otherwise you will find that both you and your dog are prey to the many diseases and illnesses that run rampant through the animal world.

It is always better to be safe than sorry, and with a good vet all lined up for your dog you can be assured that he will get the best care and attention that he deserves.

You also have the added benefit of being able to get your dog's toenails trimmed. A fact that you will much appreciate when you find yourself with claw marks on your arms when your otherwise placid dog learns that he is about to go to the vet.

Do not worry: this is not a hazard that must be faced with all dogs, just a select few of them who seem to find getting jabbed in various places on their body to be painful and naturally enough, associate it with a trip to the vet.

It's truly uncanny how they know that this is where you will be going, even if you don't say a word about it in the first place. In fact it can be difficult to even find your faithful mutt when you have to take him to the vet. You will find that your normally enthusiastic-car-rider dog has absented himself!

My first dog, Catcher, was unfortunately one of these and I have to ask, do you know how hard it is hold a wiggling 70 pounds of dog in your hands every time you have to go to the vet. I had to resort to finally putting him in his box which was hard in itself!

In the end, I purchased a toenail clipper to do the job myself. This definitely made my job easier in taking Catcher to the vet's when he had to get his shots! (I don't use the toenail clipper now as I much prefer to have someone more capable of this to do it for me!)

The added benefit of taking your dog to the vet is that you get to make sure that your dog is on the right health-wise, and if not you can always get the advice of these professionals to help you out.

Keeping Them Fed

Alpine, my Saint Bernard is a testament to the benefits of a good and healthy diet. He is also I have to say, unfortunately far more than my arms can carry these days!

But it is a fact that keeping your dog well fed is a right direction on the road to keeping him happy. Just like the old saying that the way to a man's heart is through his stomach, I would have to say that the same reasoning applies to a dog as well!

Most dogs I know, barring some watchdogs, will gladly become my friend for life if I keep a few scraps and goodies in my pockets every time I go visiting.

Keeping your dog happy through good feeding is one thing. Overfeeding them and giving them unhealthy foods however, is not the best way to keep a healthy dog.

Most importantly you might want to be aware of the effects of chocolate on a dog. The Spitz that I was talking about earlier was a much loved and pampered dog, unfortunately in this case he was too pampered and went on to develop cataracts of the eye. My friends didn't know about the effects of chocolate on a dog until it was too late.

Dogs should also not be fed most ready made meals that many of us eat on a daily basis, as well processed foods that can be found on most shelves in our households.

Other than that you will find that there are a few other no-no's that you will want to stay away from, and for these I recommend that you have a chat with your vet who can tell you better than I can what is good and what is bad, or that you refer up a book dedicated to your dog breed.

What I have mentioned here are just the most obvious things that we would feed our dogs without thinking twice about it.

You should also not overfeed your dog as this can lead to obesity and many health issues for your dog. Twice a day is normally enough to keep them healthy and happy.

Barring these restrictions you will find that feeding your dogs a good healthy, home cooked meal at least once or twice a week is much better for his system than any of the dog chow brands on the market.

The keyword in that earlier sentence was *healthy*. When I said a home cooked meal I didn't mean that you should nuke a TV dinner for your dog alongside your own TV dinner. This is not a treat, and is definitely not healthy!

If however, you don't have the time or the inclination to whip up a home cooked meal for you much less for your dog you can stick with the myriad dog food brands that you will find in the stores.

These too, you will find, come in many different varieties. Indeed, unlike the olden days when one type of dog chow was given to all types of dog large and small, short and long, these days you will find that most dog chow brands come in as many different varieties as the dogs themselves.

I can personally attest to this since I buy three separate types of dog food now, to cater for the Saint Bernard, the Chihuahua, and the Labrador. Of course I also supplement this food with cooked meals as well, but that doesn't change the fact that one corner of my larder is stacked with dog food.

The long and short of it then? For a happy dog, keep your dog fed well. For a happy and *healthy* dog, don't feed him junk food!

They Need Love and Affection Too

This shouldn't really have to be stated but I have found that sometimes plain speaking is the best thing all around, so I will say this outright. Most dogs need as much love and affection as humans do.

They are a very loving and affectionate animal, and intelligent into the bargain. They will know when you are just playing around with their affections and they will feel it deeply if you hurt their feelings.

They will also react to the different ways that you treat them, and in this I have found that they are very much like humans.

If they are angry at you they will not hesitate to show you this and will in many cases display this with a show of temper or a tantrum. And of course, just like humans, the older some dogs get, the more tempered they become and the less likely to show their anger.

If you do something to hurt their feelings, they will show this too. You can sometimes drown in the sorrow you see in their eyes, and I have to say that this goes right to my heart. It is with great difficulty that I managed to train them at all!

This is also one of the reasons that I don't favor Basset Hounds. It would be almost impossible for me to live the constant soulful glances!

You will definitely know when your dog is happy as he will show you in no uncertain manner, and you can be assured that you will know when he's feeling left out and ignored.

They will almost always try and get your attention if you're in the vicinity and they're feeling lonely. And trust me, you won't be in any doubt that what they want is your undivided attention!

They will feel it down to their doggy hearts when you have to break routine and go away for some time, and they will be the first to greet you with great enthusiasm when you come back.

If they want to play and frisk about like a puppy again, you will be dragged this way and that until you give in and indulge in your younger feelings as well.

And if you show a preference to someone or something else leaving them excluded for any length of time, they can display signs of jealousy and sometimes dejection.

Most of all though, if you treat them right and look after them with loving care and affection, you will find that they will give you their unstinting love and affection back.

They will even follow you unquestioningly to the ends of the earth regardless of their own well being. At that point, it's *your* duty to them, to turn them back for their own safety.

Having a dog is a two way street on the heart strings, and both you and your dog can become deeply affected by each other.

As the leader, (at this point, the term "owner" seems redundant) you will have to be the stronger of the two and make decisions that are best for you and your dog.

There's nothing else on this earth like the devotion that a dog will show to you if only you treat him right.

Grooming Issues

Since I have already touched upon the subject of dog grooming, I will go through it only very lightly in this section. This was done more in the way of getting you acquainted with the many things that you need to look into once you finally have your dog.

To that extent grooming your dog is a very important part of the entire process. Grooming in this case doesn't include only brushing his coat, but also includes bathing as well as brushing their teeth (or what passes for that in the doggy world), trimming their toenails etc., etc.

Depending mainly on the breed of dog that you have, you will find that your grooming duties vary. As mentioned earlier, some dogs require extensive grooming, while with others you can get away with the minimum required grooming needs.

If you have the need for it, and you have the monetary means to indulge yourself, you could if you wanted to give over this task to a professional grooming service.

That is of course if you find this task to be too onerous to do yourself, or if you have a need to do it everyday. Naturally not everyone can afford the services of a professional grooming service on a daily or even weekly or monthly basis.

Because of this, some people instead take their dogs to these grooming services on an annual basis or at suitably spaced intervals.

Most other people however, prefer to groom their dogs themselves. These people, like me, I'm sure prefer to have a personal hand in the grooming process.

I find that I derive a great satisfaction from seeing a clean shiny coat. Not that it lasts too long. Before the day is out both of the dogs have found, and jumped and rolled around in every dirt patch and mud hole that exists in our neighborhood. The Labrador is a little more dignified and only rolls around in half of the mud holes!

Like I said, the grooming process doesn't only involve brushing the dog's coat. It includes bathing the dog as well as sundry other things. These sundry other things includes, getting their teeth cleaned on a regular basis as well.

This can be done either by yourself using one of the many products that exists in the market these days or by your vet, or a grooming service.

Admittedly this particular task isn't too easy if your dog insists on wriggling around the entire time so you might want to consider giving this over to someone who is better able to handle this task.

The same thing applies to trimming the dog's toenails. You will find that as time goes if you don't get the toenails trimmed regularly that not only will your dog be liable to scratch and hurt you, but he can also hurt himself without realizing it.

I don't attend to this task by myself as I live in the fear that I will get too close to the cuticle, but instead give it over to the vet to do it along with a thorough cleaning of the ears and teeth!

When You Have to Go Away

Unless you do this on a daily basis you will find that when you go away for any length of time, your dog will feel it down to his doggy toes.

This is one of the factors that you needed to take into account when you were looking for the right dog for you. So if you are leaving the dog alone for any appreciable length of time daily, you should have chosen a dog that can acclimatize to this fact.

If on the other hand, your going away has to do with vacations or emergencies, or work related wanderings that are very rare, then you will have to find a suitable means for your dog to be looked after while you are away.

If you have family or friends who can spare the time, and with whom your dog is familiar, this is one of your better choices. You can easily leave your dog with any of these people and not have to face too many worries.

For any dog however, the time that you are away is always a problem. Dogs are creatures of habit and your going away leaves a great big gaping hole in their lives.

Dogs also live for the now, not in the past or for the future, but for the moment, so when their routines are messed up they tend to react to this.

Some dogs react by destroying everything in their paths (with this in mind I have renamed my little Chihuahua, Destroyer).

Other dogs will slink away to a corner and pine away.

The eight year old Labrador that I have, is of this mind. If ever I need to go away for a day or two, she pines away and refuses to eat. This is a form of separation anxiety and I do my best to make up for this. Since I got her from a shelter who knows what her life was like before this.

Some dogs will take things prosaically and not display any outward signs of missing you, but you can be sure that when you get back home that you will get an enthusiastic, and in the case of Alpine, a slobbering welcome.

And all of this despite the fact that I have arranged the best care for them. I'm lucky in that my family and friends will come over to check up on my dogs when I'm not there and see to their various needs.

This means that I can leave them at home with no worries. Otherwise I would have to take up one of the other options, and these I feel would not go down very well with my canine friends.

Unfortunately, most people are not as fortunate as I am, and have to resort to the other options.

These include the more popular methods of getting a dog sitter, but if your dog is temperamental then the last thing you want to do is to leave it in the care of someone he doesn't know, and someone who doesn't know too much about dogs.

If your dog sitter is the kid next door, or even two doors down, who knows your dog, knows dogs, and is responsible, then that's another matter entirely.

Otherwise I would suggest you think about taking your dog with you where you're going. This is not too difficult if you're just going cross country to visit Mom and get some of her turkey dinners.

But if you're going away on holiday out of the country, or you're going on a business trip, then you will find that it is impossible to take your dog along with you.

Your other option, and this is an ever popular option, is to leave the dog with professional sitters. Think of it something along the lines of a doggy Club Med.

They get all the care and attention that they deserve, and you have the knowledge and the security that your dog is being looked after by people who know what they're doing, and who know about dogs and their various needs.

With this last option you can be assured that your dog is getting the best care, and who knows, he might not even want to come back home!

Not All Dogs are the Same

The title of this section, and everything that I have said up to this point tells you what that you need to know about this section. Not all dogs are the same.

You can take two dogs of the same breed, same age, even better, from the same litter, and you will get two distinctly different dogs.

In this aspect as well, they are like humans. They have their own identities and their own quirks and eccentricities. A lifetime is generally not long enough to get to know your dog well. You will be learning little bits and pieces about him until the very last.

This is on a deeper level however than most of us are

willing to go. What I was really trying to get to with this section was that the way you treat your dog will to a great extent depend on the breed of the dog.

You can't use the same grooming methods, exercise routines, food needs and other needs for a Spaniel that you would for a Wolfhound. Their needs are too different for you to use the same techniques on each of the dogs.

You will need to go through and find out what is best for your dog breed before you apply any of the knowledge that your friends and other dog loving people, might have given you. They might have a toy dog breed variety for a pet and you might have a purebred Bulldog for a pet.

The two different varieties need vastly different things from you and if you're getting a dog, you will need to step up to that particular plate and bat a wining hand. That might be mixing my metaphors in a large way, but hopefully it conveyed the message.

At the time when you get your dog itself, you need to ask the people you're getting the dog from, what the various basic needs of your dog are.

If you're getting a dog from a pet store, the basic needs will like as not, be the same across the board for all of the dogs. But if you're getting a purebred dog you will want to find out if there are any special needs that you will have to know about. Here too, you will most likely find that the basic needs are the same.

It's only when you get more breed specific and you need to go deeper into things that you will find there are specific needs that you have to look into and take care of.

A Last Word

There are many reasons why a person would choose a dog as a pet, but in the end I believe it comes down to one of two things: either you're a dog person or you're not. And it really is as simple as that.

But if you want to go into specifics, one of the main reasons why a person would choose a dog as a pet over a cat, or a bird or even a cobra is probably because a dog will bond more easily with their human companions than otherwise.

This is why choosing your dog is such a crucial matter and why you really should go through the process if you can. Of course if you just bond immediately with a dog on sight, all of these questions and choices won't make any difference.

It won't matter what breed he is, or what color, what height, or even what his characteristics are, you've bonded with your dog and that's that.

In the end this is really why people look to have a dog as a pet. The companionship that a dog will give them is what most of us look forward to, and we know that if treat them right, our dogs will become our loyal and faithful companions, and in the end it really is as simple as all that.

Where to Buy this Book

You can buy this book on Amazon. Just go to amazon.com (or your local Amazon site if available) and search for "Choosing A Dog Breed Guide by Eric Nolah" or just "Eric Nolah".

You can also order it at any bookstore if they don't have it in stock. Just give them the IBSN below:

ISBN 978-0-9866004-5-6

Latest Books by Psylon Press

Dog Breeds Pictures
By Eric Nolah
ISBN 978-0-9866004-6-3

Cute Puppy Pictures
By Eric Nolah
ISBN 978-0-9866004-7-0

100% Blonde Jokes
By R. Cristi
ISBN 978-0-9866004-1-8

www.ingramcontent.com/pod-product-compliance
Lightning Source LLC
LaVergne TN
LVHW021501080426
835509LV00018B/2364